Kochanski's
Concertina Beer Hall
— THE RETURN OF ROCKABILLY —

It started on a dare. In October of 2009 (my now wife) Colleen and I were having coffee at the Hi-Fi Café on Kinnickinnic Avenue (Milwaukee, WI) and I saw a poster on the wall for "rockabilly" music at a place called Kochanski's Concertina Beer Hall. My mind filled with questions: "Rockabilly?", "Could this be true?", "Has it possibly returned?" My auditory channels replayed low-fidelity and scratchy cortical recordings of Jorris Hennessee, Sterling Kelly, Bud Landon, Ked Killen and other long and almost forgotten "ghost wails". When have I last heard rockabilly? It had been a long, too long, time.

I could not place the address but assumed it to be in a rough neighborhood. "Do you want to go there?" I asked. Colleen replied at once, "Sure!" So we went.

As we approached the brick building I recalled that a few years before, this had been Art Altenburg's Concertina Bar and I had actually been there. Though skeptical about what it was going to be like, we saw a young woman with a flower in her hair and a gleam in her eye approaching the entrance rapidly with the demeanor of someone who did not want to miss one moment of enjoyment. We fell in love with Kochanski's at once. Present day rockabilly is even better now, as compared to how I remembered it. Colleen and I "flew our magic carpet" to Kochanski's almost every weekend for at least four months. We so much enjoyed the people and the music. I enjoyed the photographic challenge, it was like capturing imagery from the interior of a grotto.

Andy Kochanski has kept many aspects of Art Altenburg's old establishment intact and still has a polka night. The senior patrons of Altenburg's have been retained and can easily out-dance me. Some of them even come in on non-Polka nights to enjoy the rockabilly music.

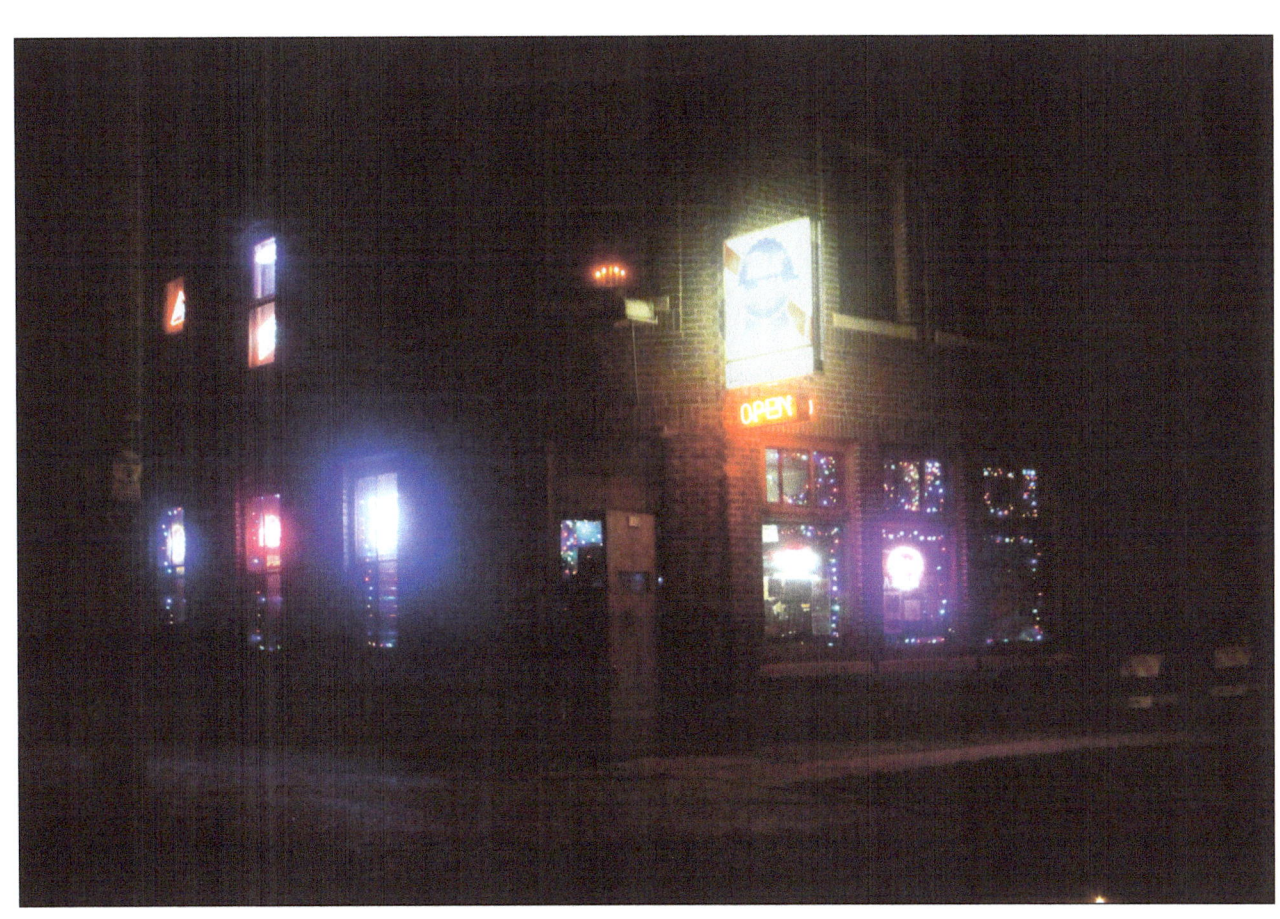

The building was built in 1900, when everything around it was celery fields. The downstairs having the bar and the upstairs containing a rooming house, which at some point was a brothel and then later was used as union offices for the factories that grew out of the farm fields that were directly across the street.

As with many of the taverns from the good ol' days, music was a part of the bar life, just as it is still here today. Within the confines of these walls, polka, was and is still part of the driving force that makes this institution what it is today. The musical genres have been expanded to include Rockabilly, Blues, Bluegrass, Country and Western, Honky-tonk, Punk, and of course Surf music. With the musical expansion, lots more people are given the opportunity to   come and enjoy this place.

I purchased, or more like saved, this place in 2007, where I continue and enhance the traditions that made this place a favorite destination for hip locals and adventurous out-of-towners who want to experience places that are truly unique and unforgettable. I hear from bands and people alike, that this place gives off a great vibe. And it does!

People who are in the know bring "virgins" here for the "WOW" factor. I know I did before I bought it. It would always bring a smile to my face when they would say "how the hell do you even know about this place."

This place represents what makes Milwaukee, Milwaukee. Good beer, great music, and most importantly, hard working people who enjoy having an extremely good time.

Even though this building gives off a special vibe, if it wasn't for friends and family who have helped me, the very talented bands that play here, and the wonderful people that come here; this place would just be an old building.

Hope to see you soon.

Andy Kochanski
fumg
www.beer-hall.com

The Bar

A winter scene with colored "Christmas lights" in the window. The audience was getting ready for the band's performance. Of note here is the man with the cigar. This was the year prior to the city of Milwaukee's ban on smoking inside of a tavern or restaurant.

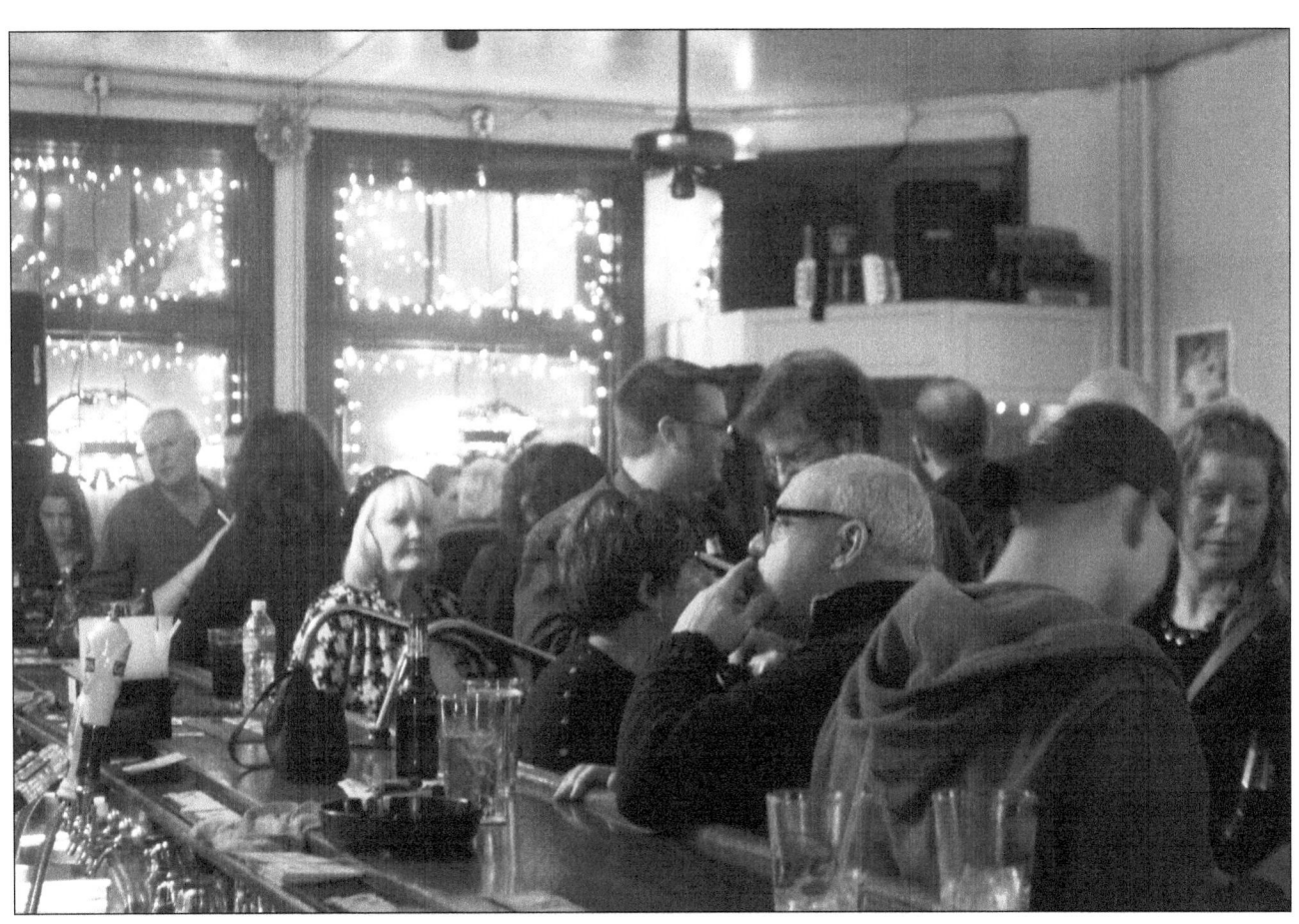

Crazy Rocket Fuel

This is the lead singer, Kari Bloom from the all female band "Crazy Rocket Fuel". Talent and dynamism sufficient to color a black & white publication. I don't know how they do it. Their music "cooks" yet their talent remains "raw".

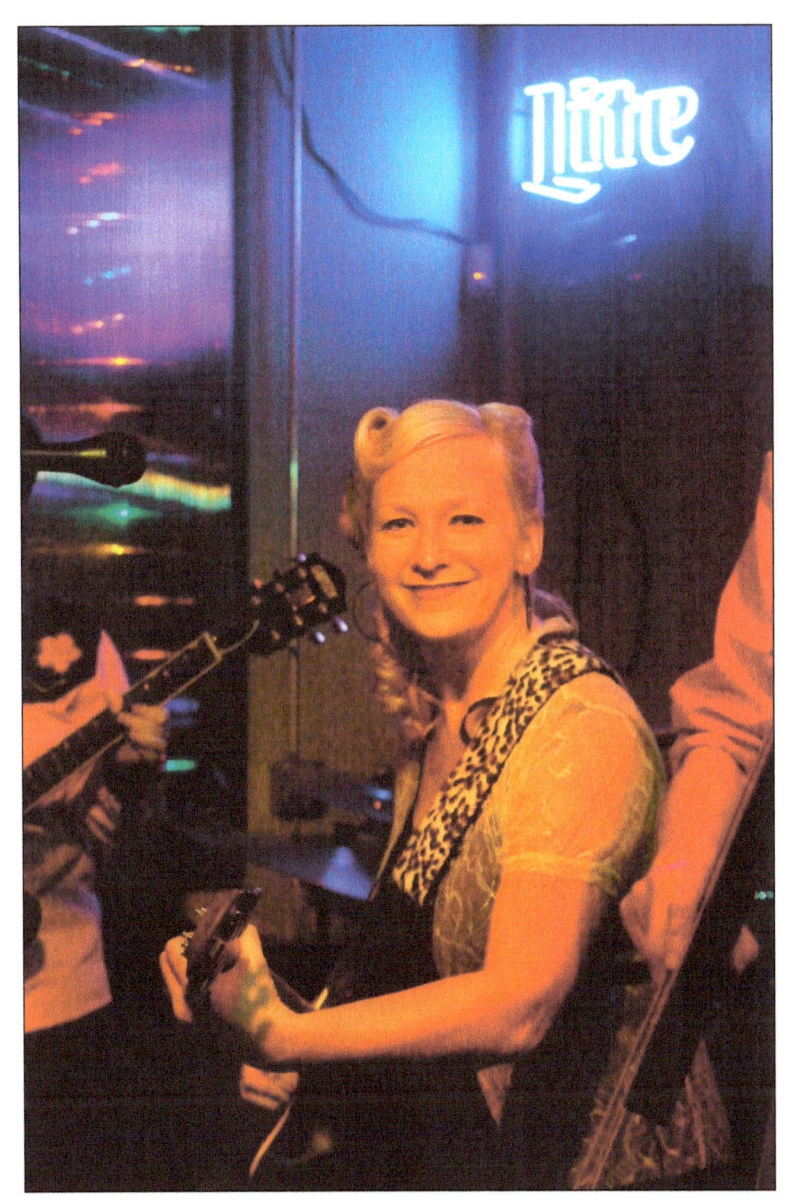

Matt Tyner

Matt is the singer and guitar player for "The Carpetbaggers". No one can play a guitar like Matt. On stage he refers to himself as Matt "MF" Tyner. What does "MF" stand for? Somehow I think it does not stand for "mighty fine", but I assure you, he is.

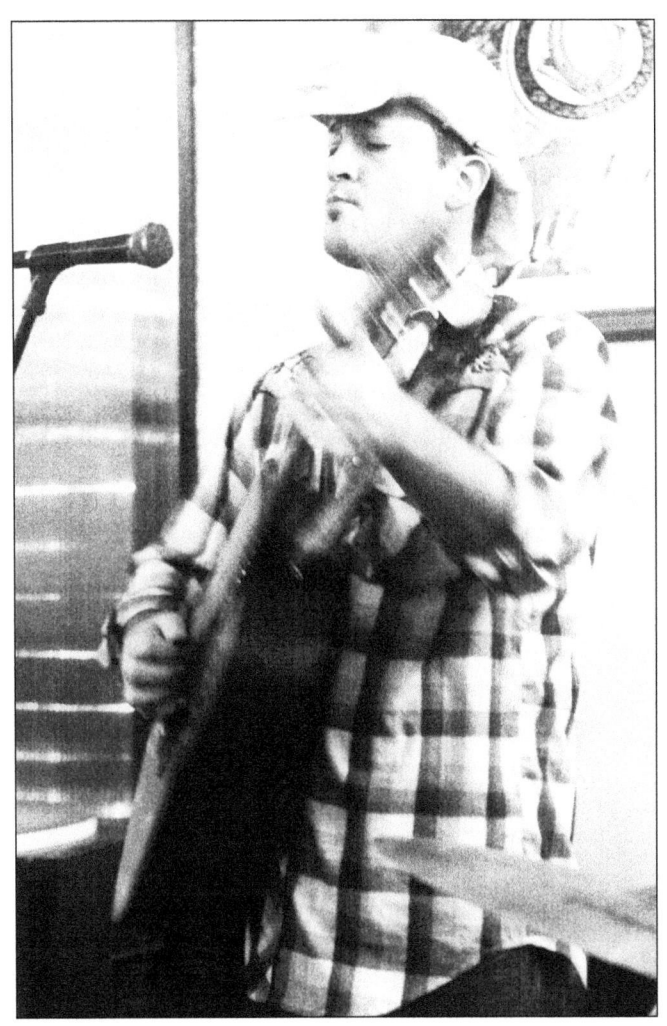

Matt Tyner

Matt Tyner Eyes closed. Cigarette dangling. Ash about to fall off.

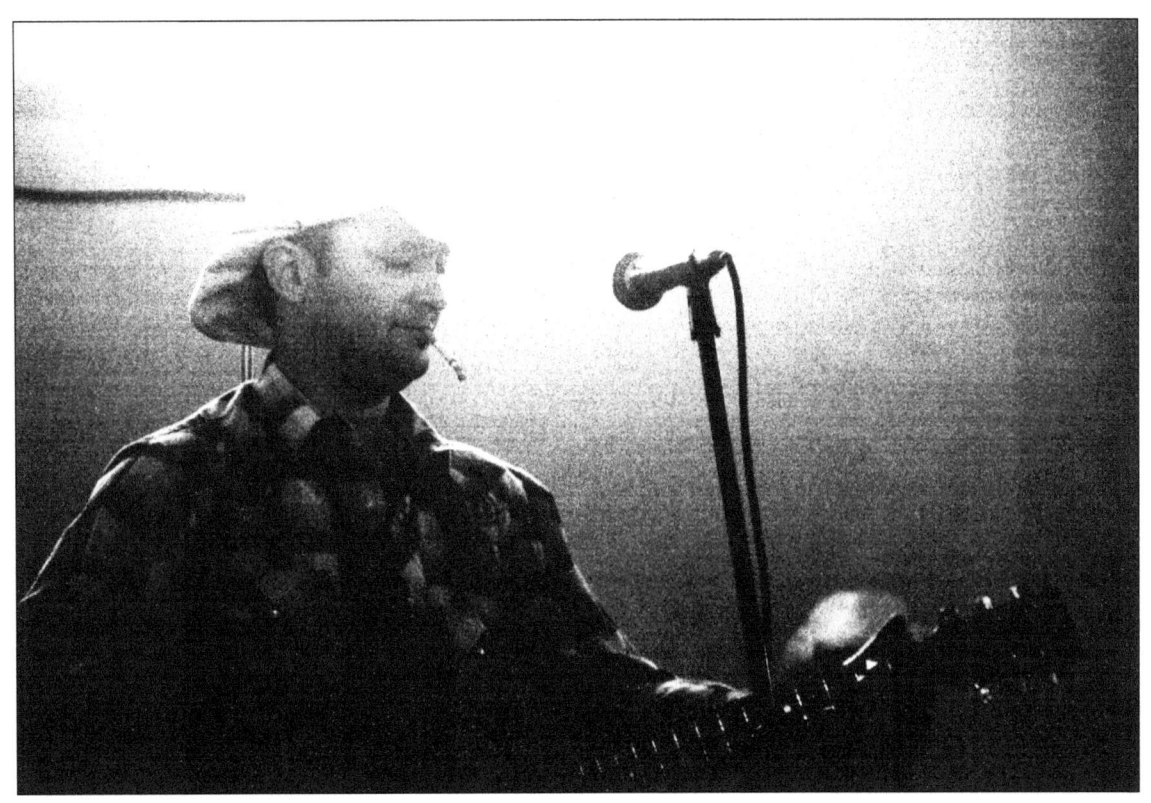

Matt Tyner

Here is a view of Matt and his "one of a kind guitar".
You don't see too many of 'em.

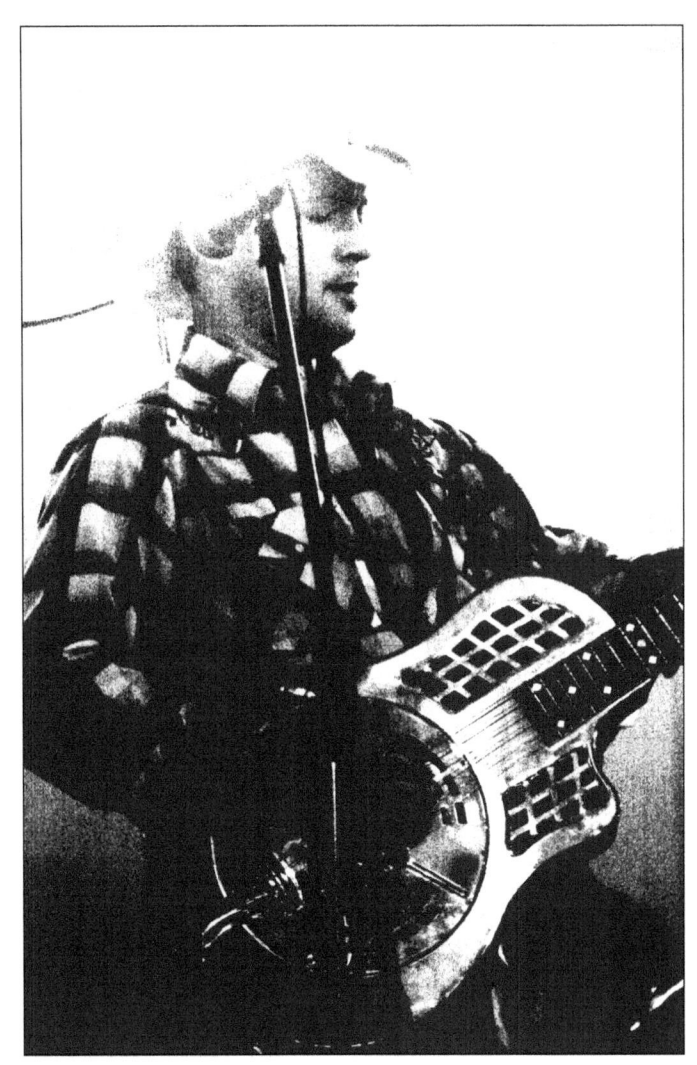

Kent Knapp

Sometimes refers to himself as "the Colonel". He is one of the "Carpetbaggers". He is a blacksmith, large and muscular. No one can get a bass to resonate the way he does.

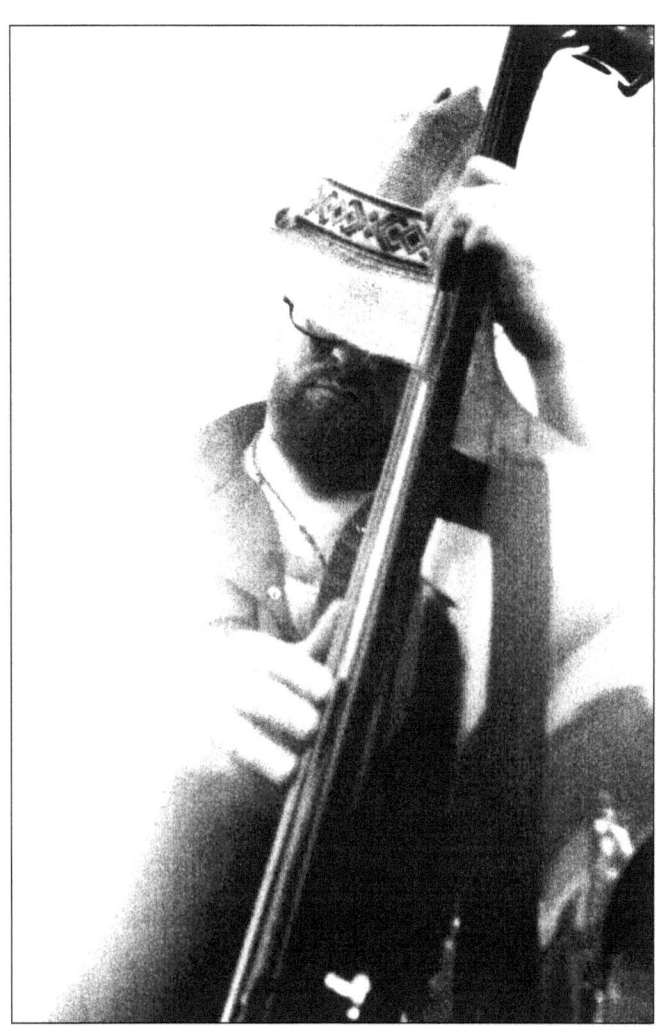

Couple

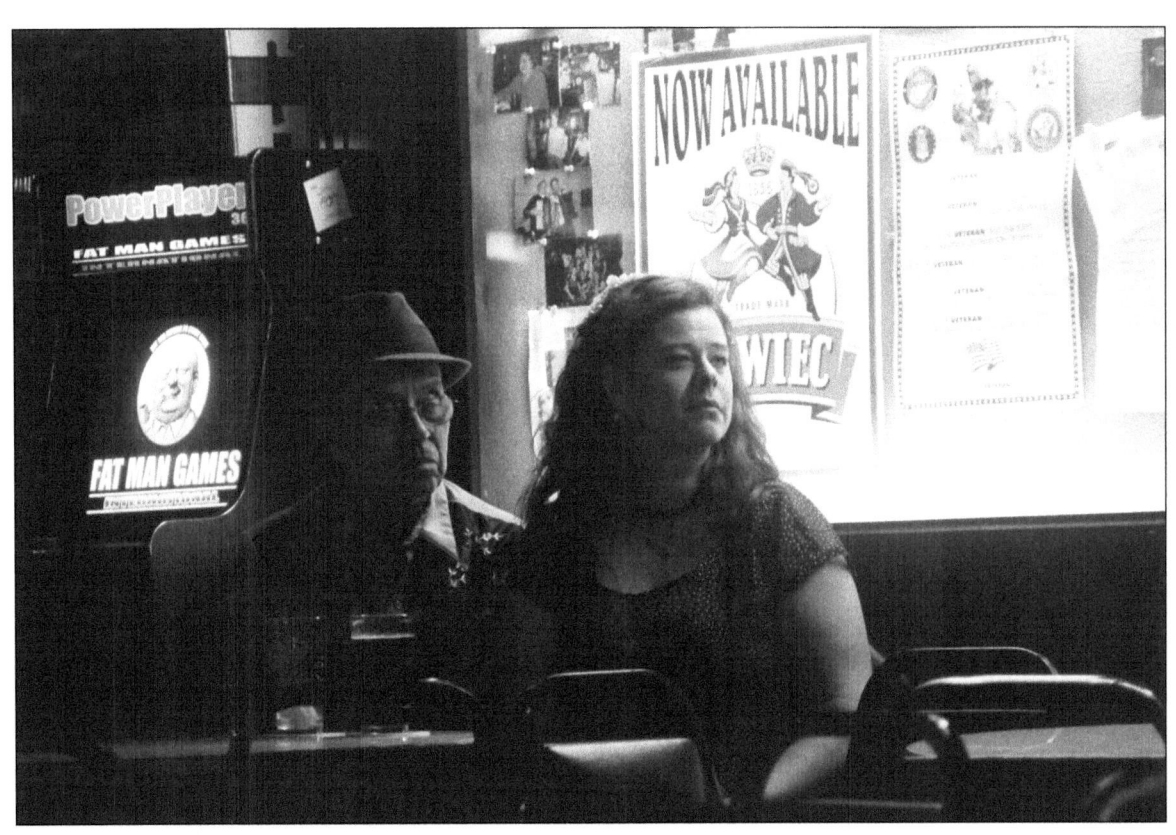

Brew City Bombshells

Kochanski's is famous for having two bands performing on weekends and "battling it out". The night I did this photography, the featured band was "Crazy Rocket Fuel", but instead of having a second band, Andy brought in a burlesque act. Though the audience had paid to hear two bands there were no complaints when the "Bombshells" appeared and pretty much but not quite "took it all off".

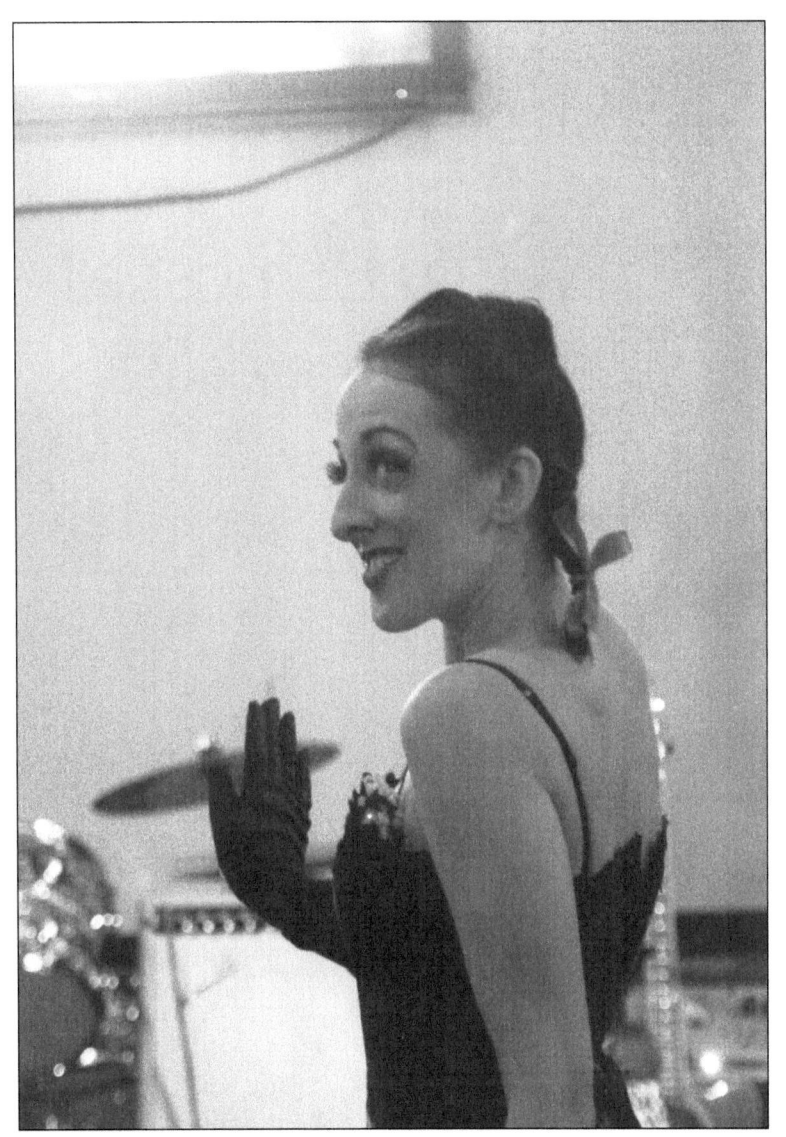

A Brew City Bombshell

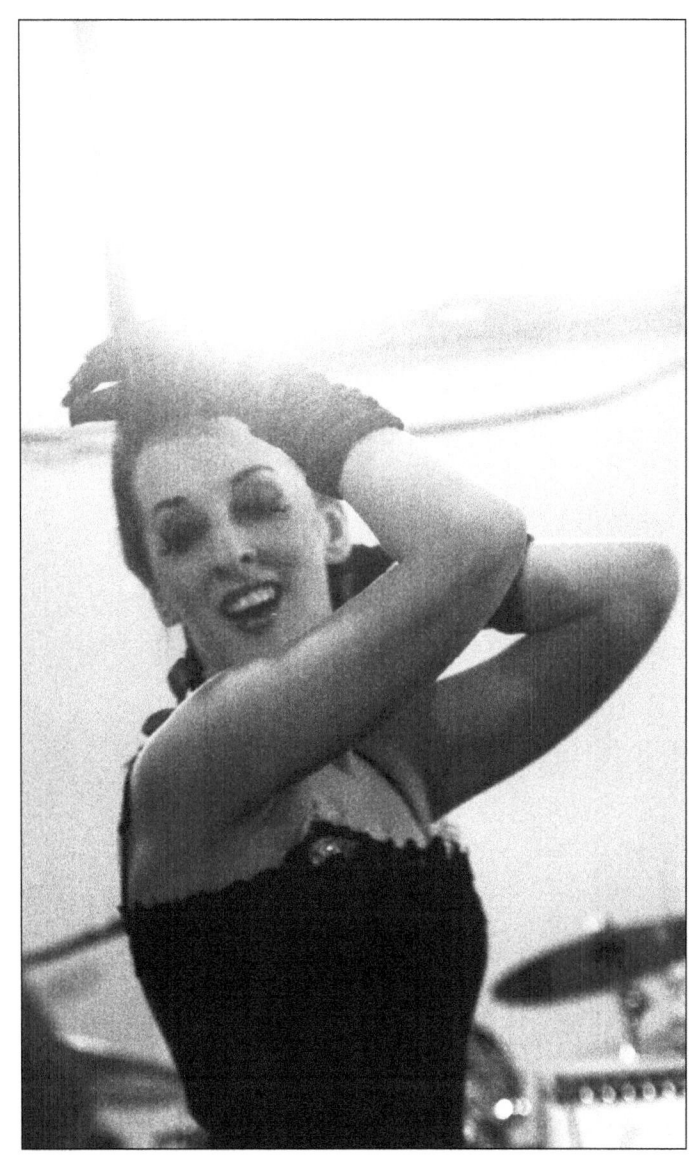

Raven Nevermore

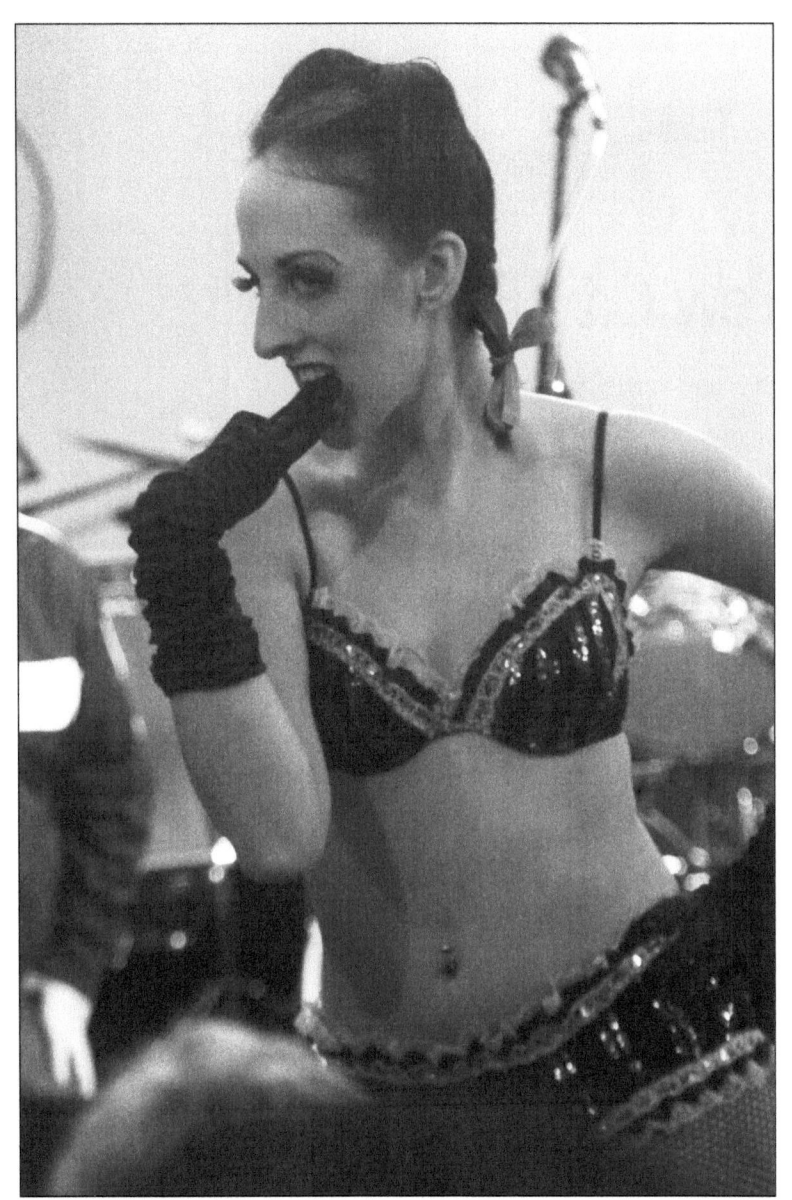

Brew City Bombshell

(With a guy in the background)

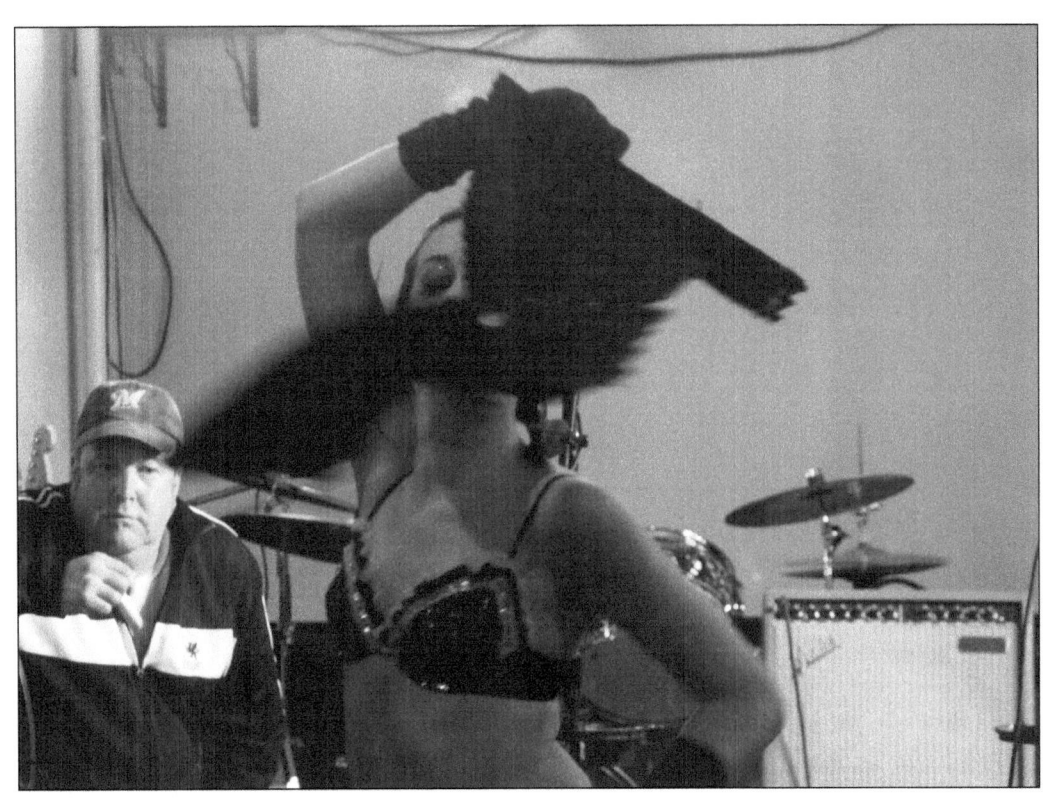

Brush Cut

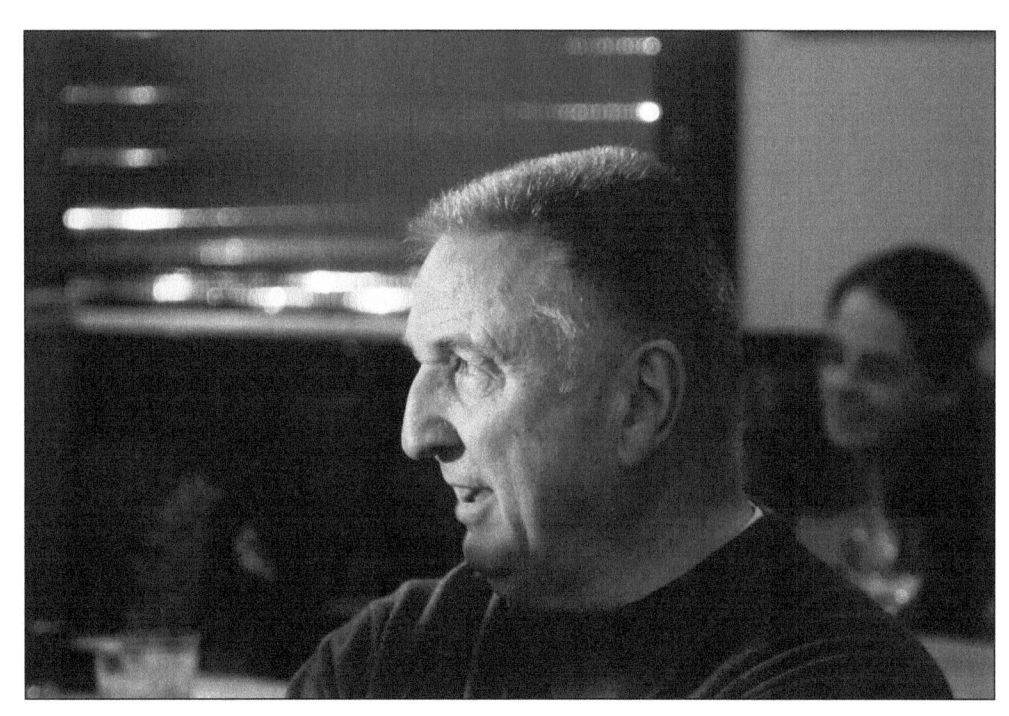

Delilah DeWylde and the Lost Boys

From Saugatuck, Michigan, Delilah with drummer D.J. McCoy and guitarist Lee Harvey made the drive to Milwaukee that night. I bought their CD and have listened to it hundreds of times. I pray they return to Milwaukee.

My apologies to "D.J" however, who I sort of lost in this photo.

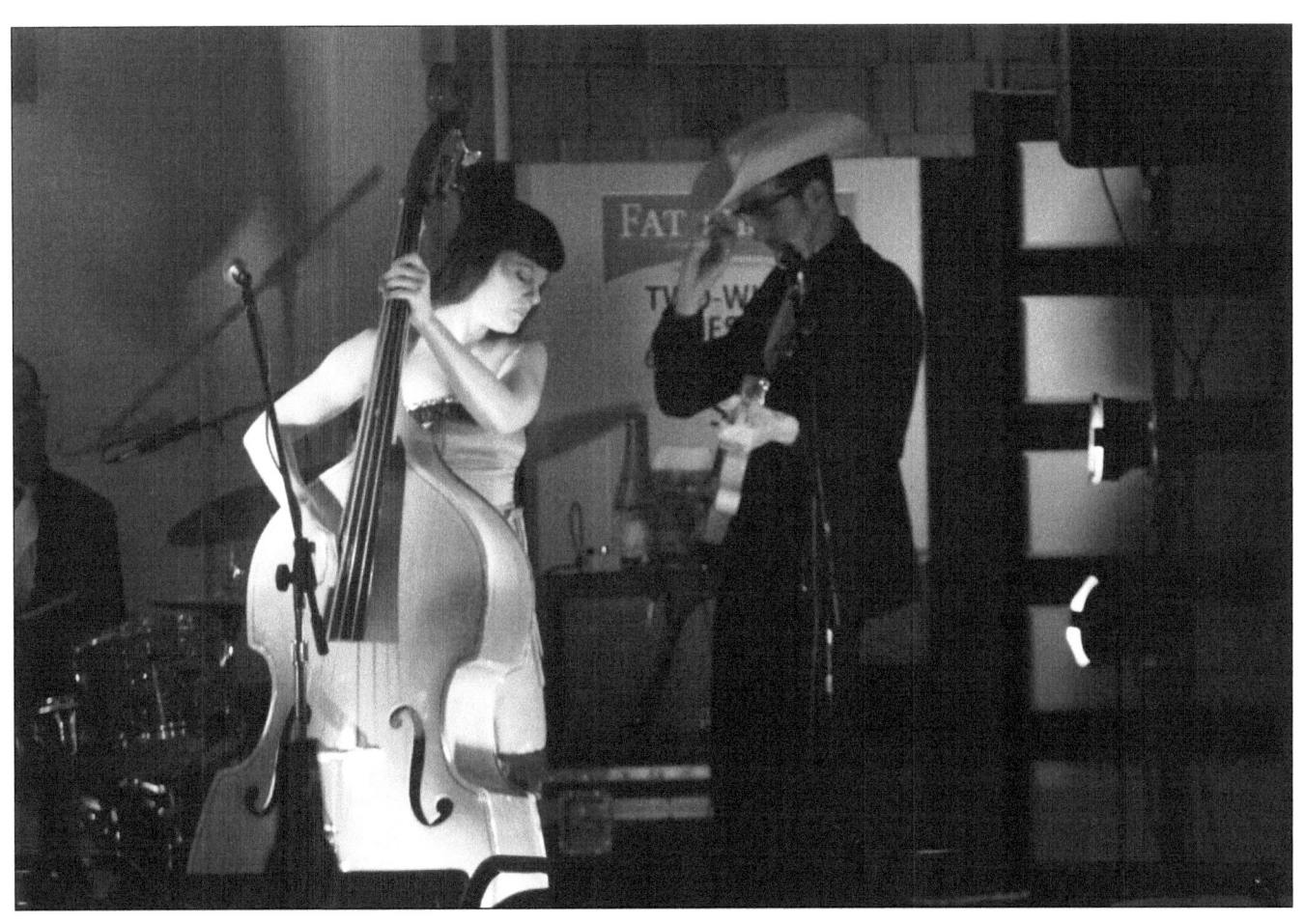

Delilah DeWylde

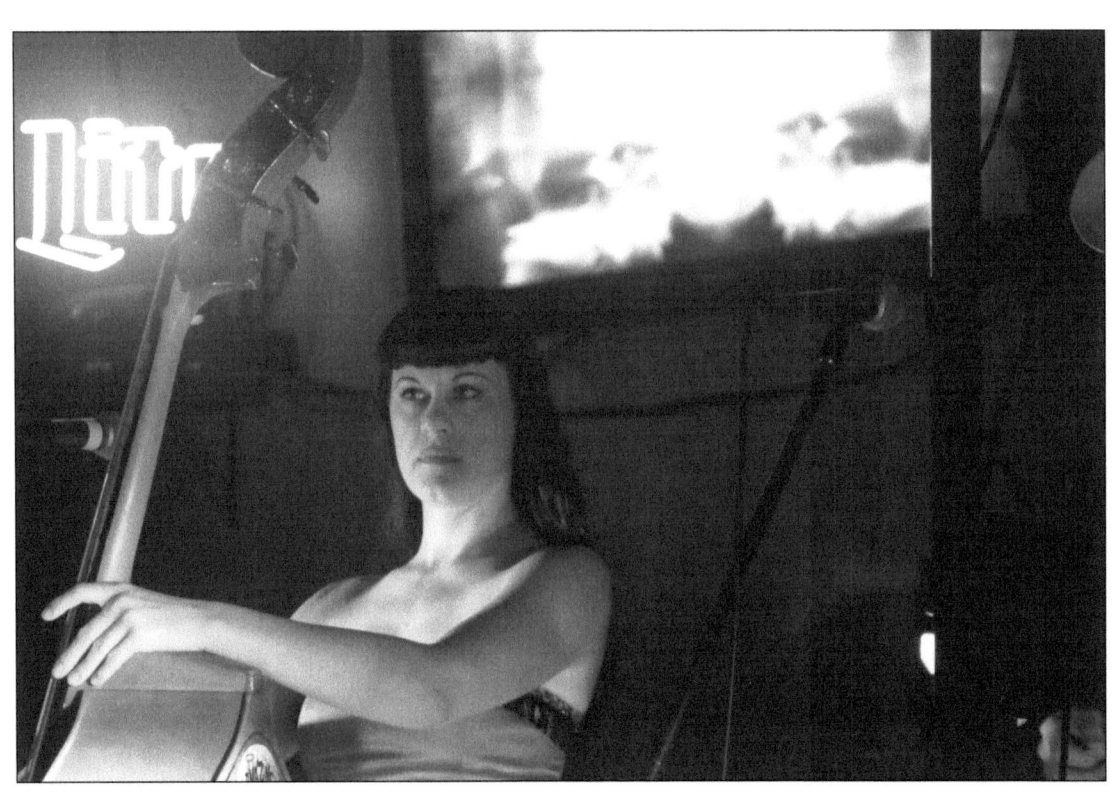

Delilah and her Bass

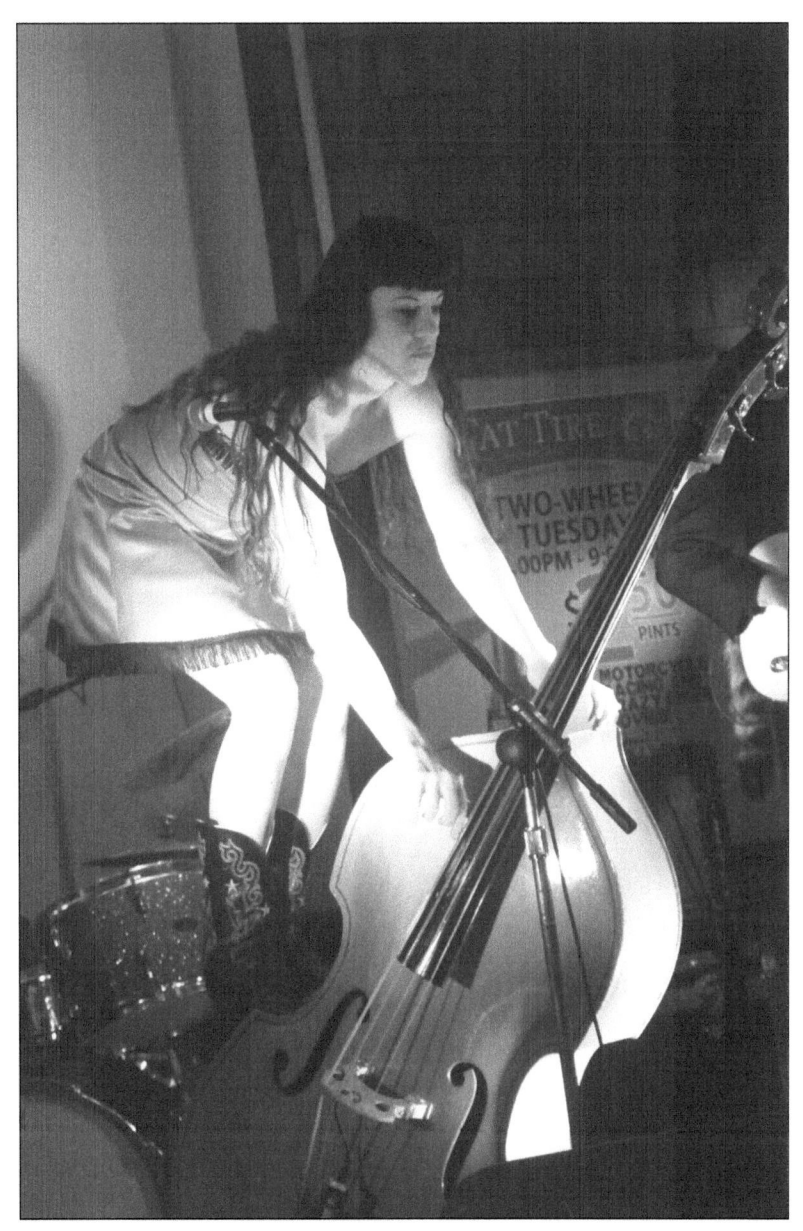

Delilah

One of my favorite photos.

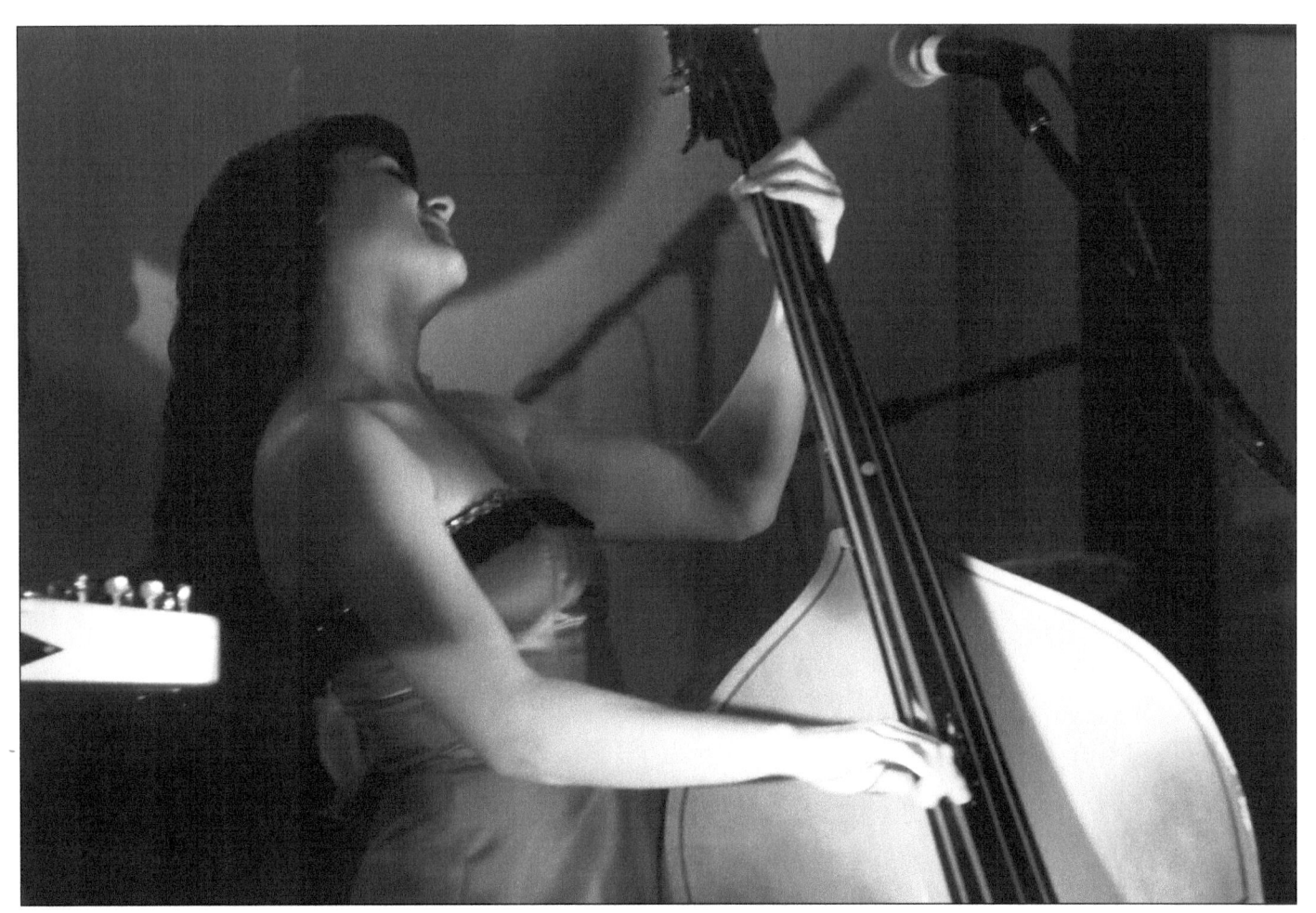

Eyes and Hand

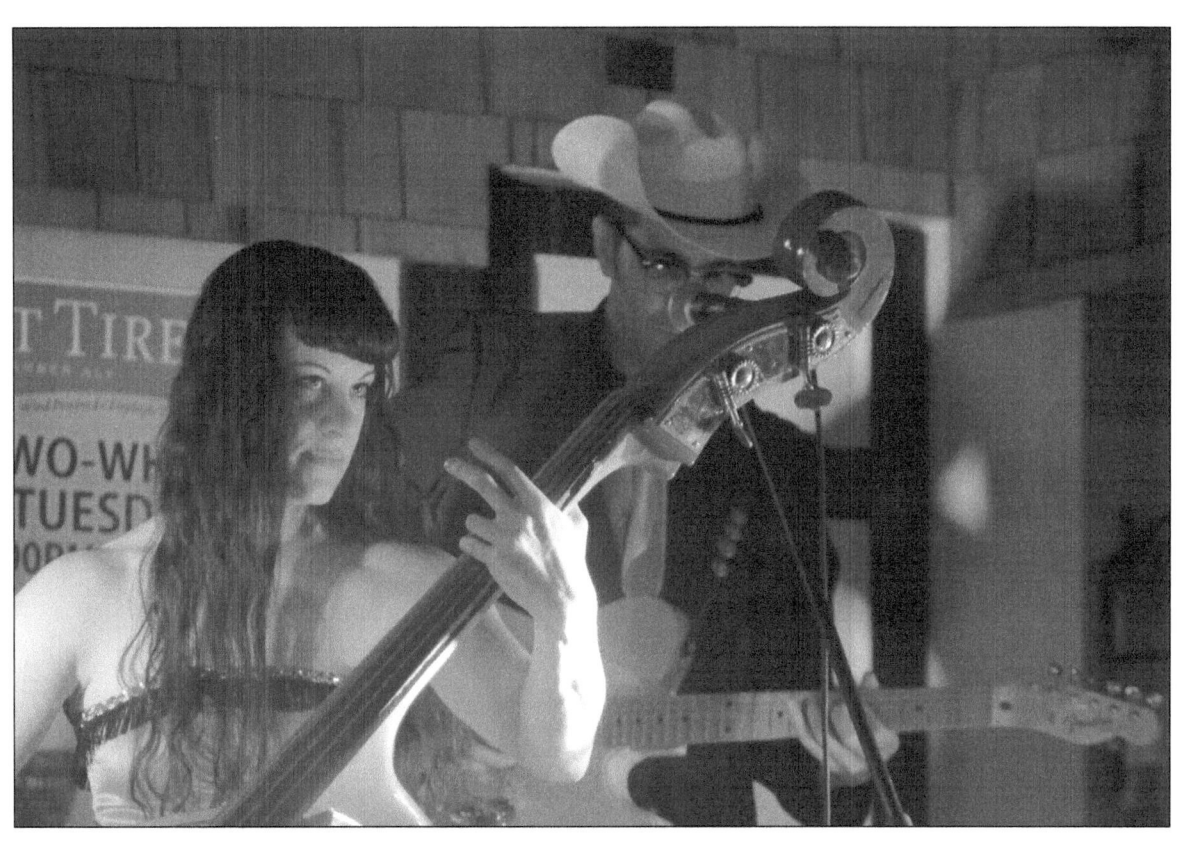

Fat Tire

Yep, another shot of Delilah but I needed a different title here.

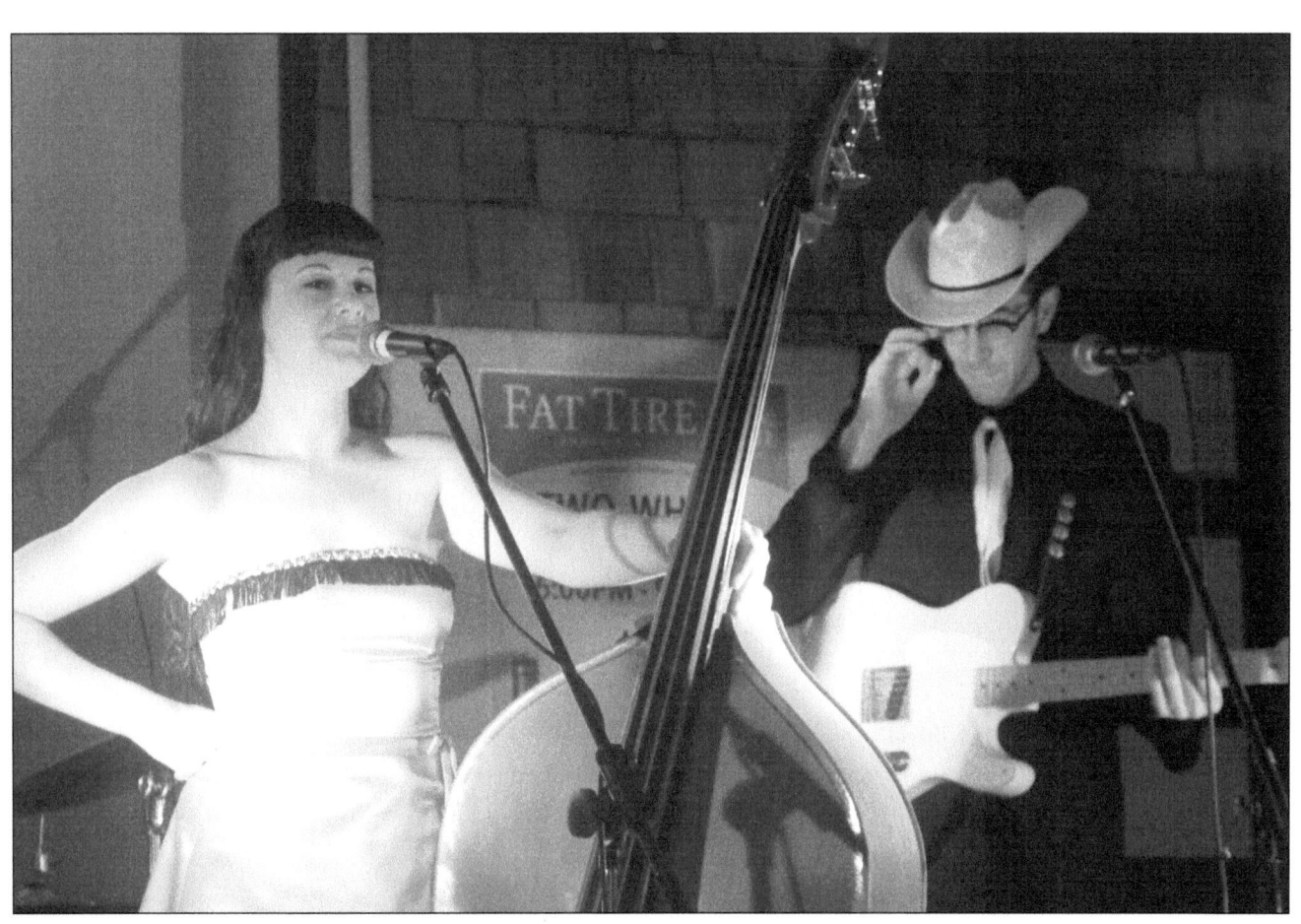

Sweet Delilah

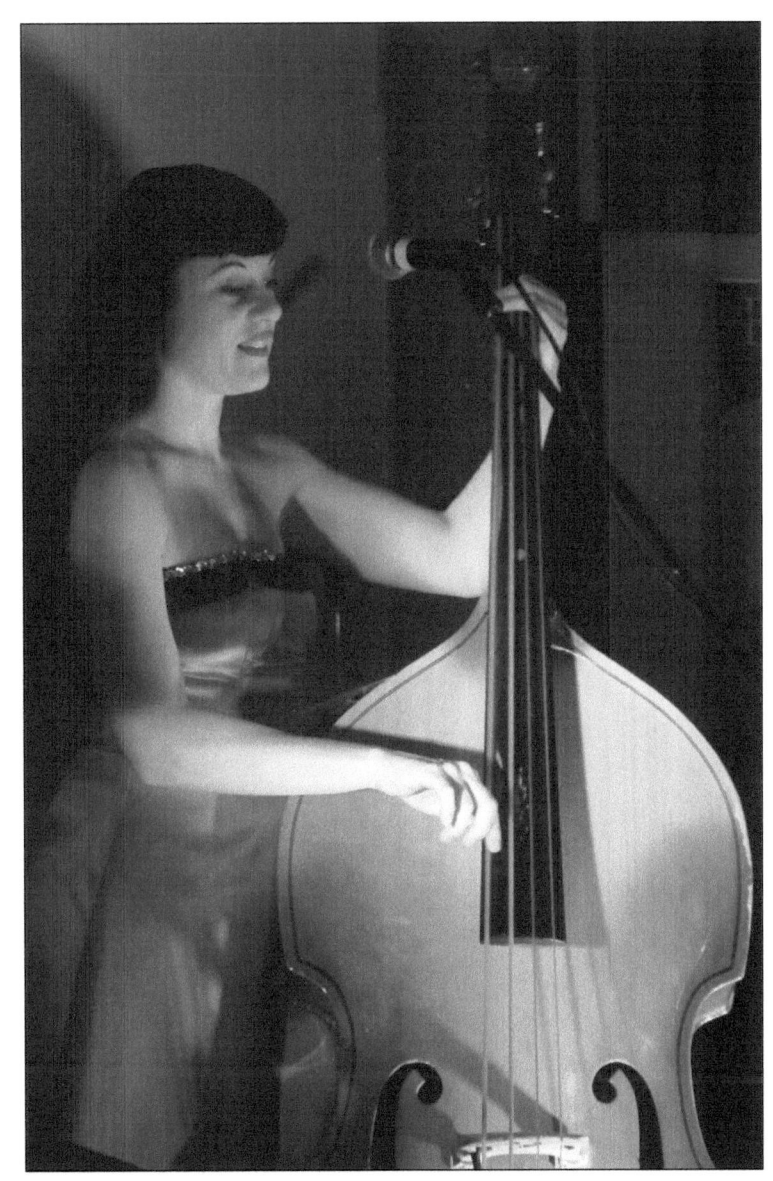

Woooooooooooooooeeeeeeeeeeee

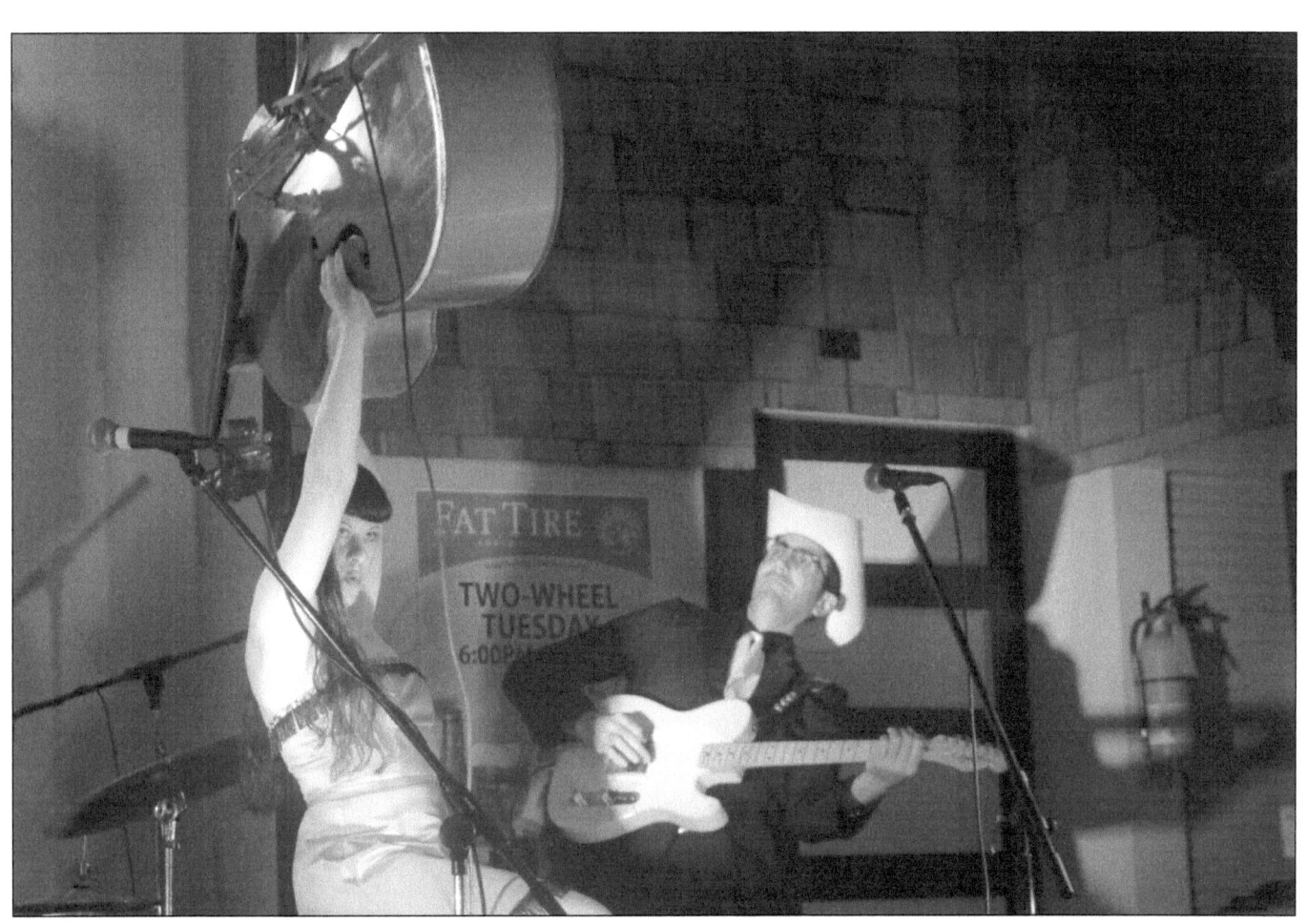

Beer Drinker

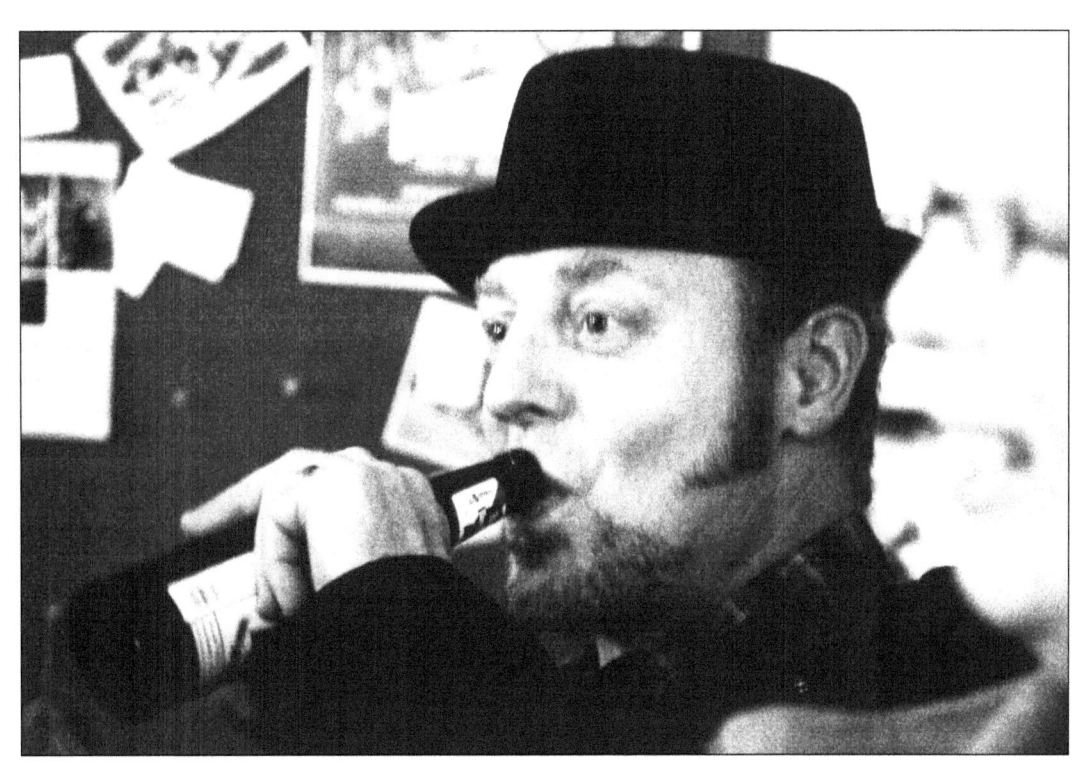

Mary Rogers from the Uptown Savages

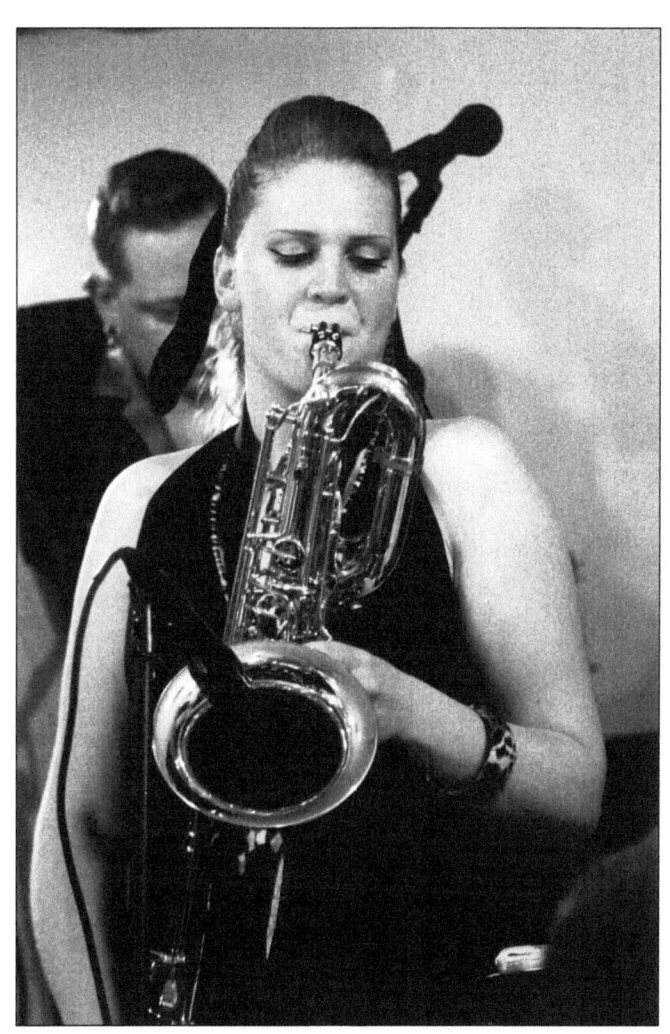

Untitled

Documentation of the last cigarette legally smoked indoors within a city of Milwaukee tavern.

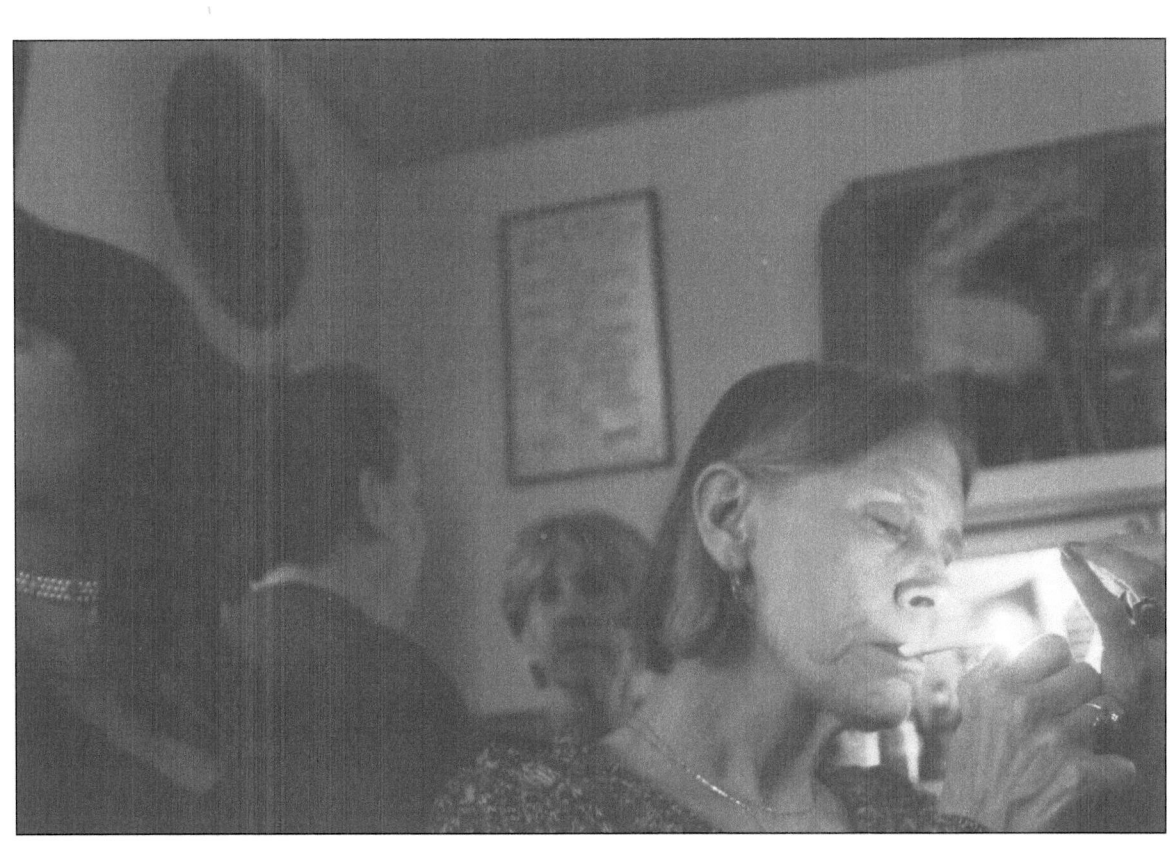

The Flower Girl Lady

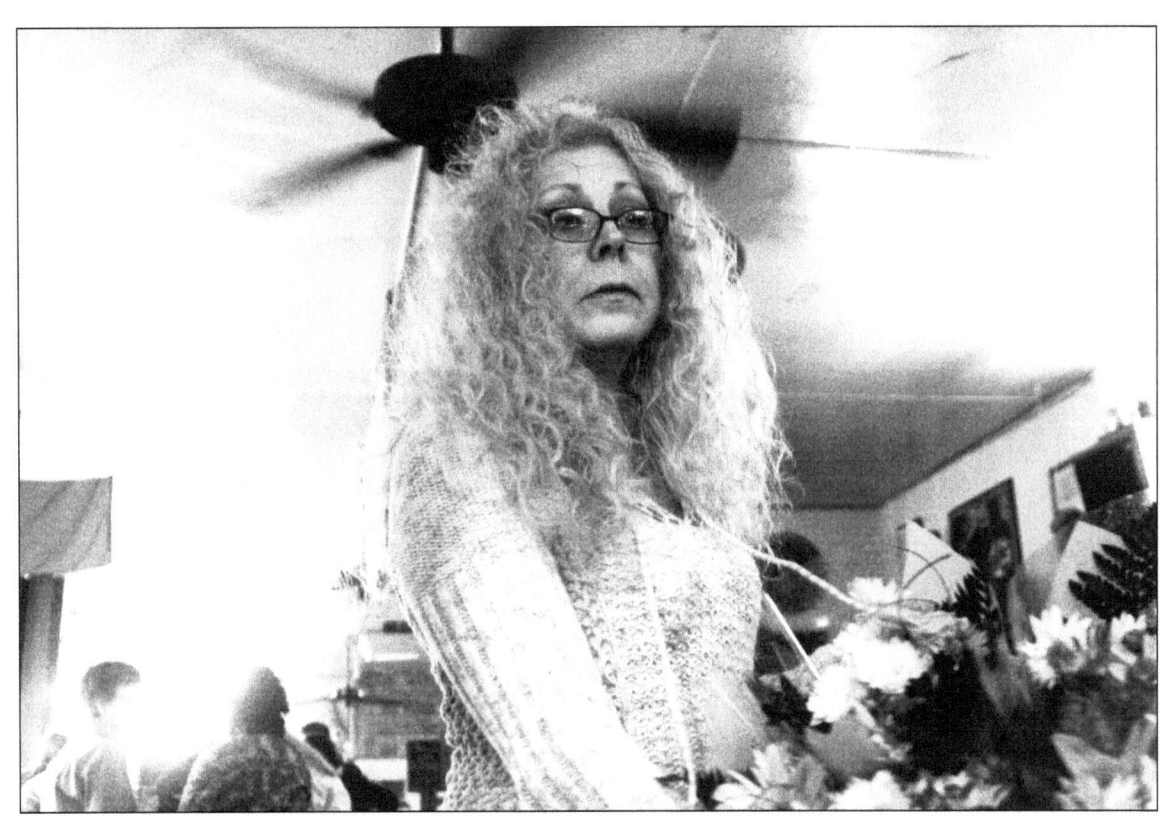

Colleen

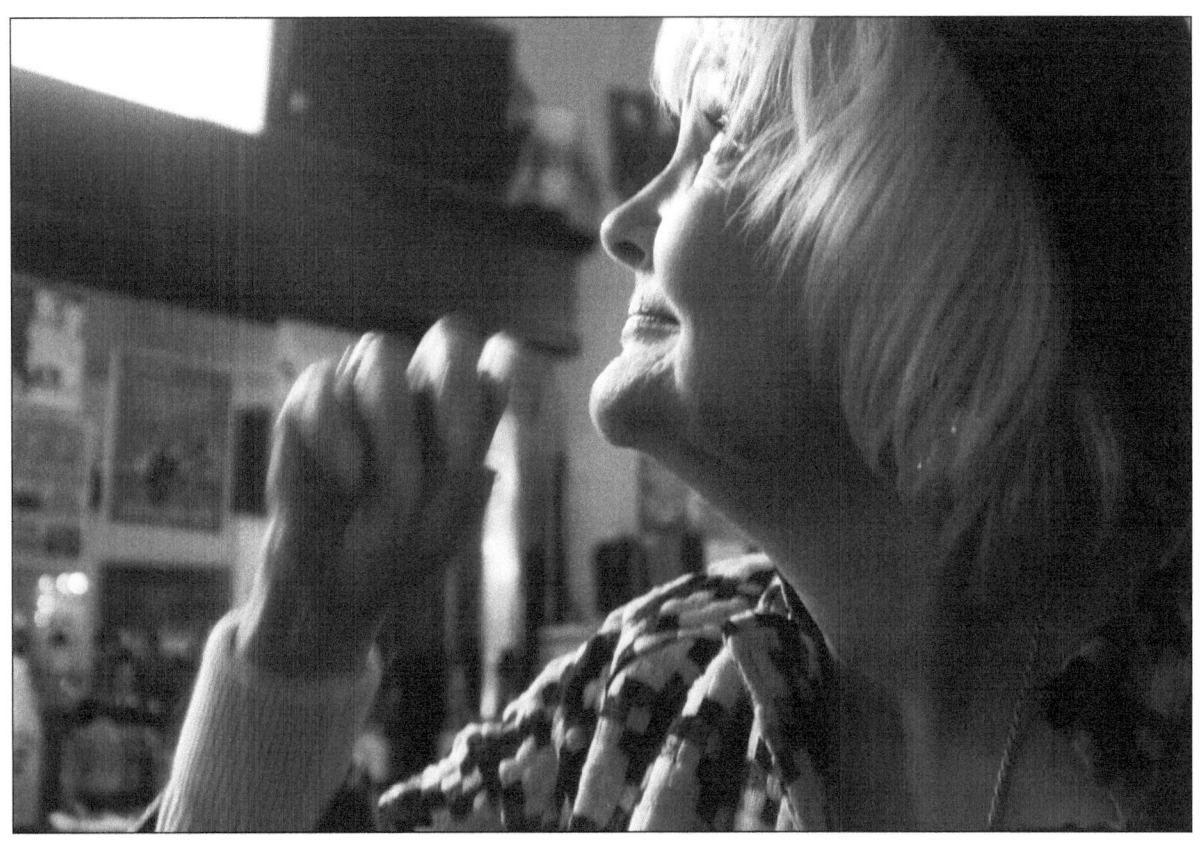

Girls

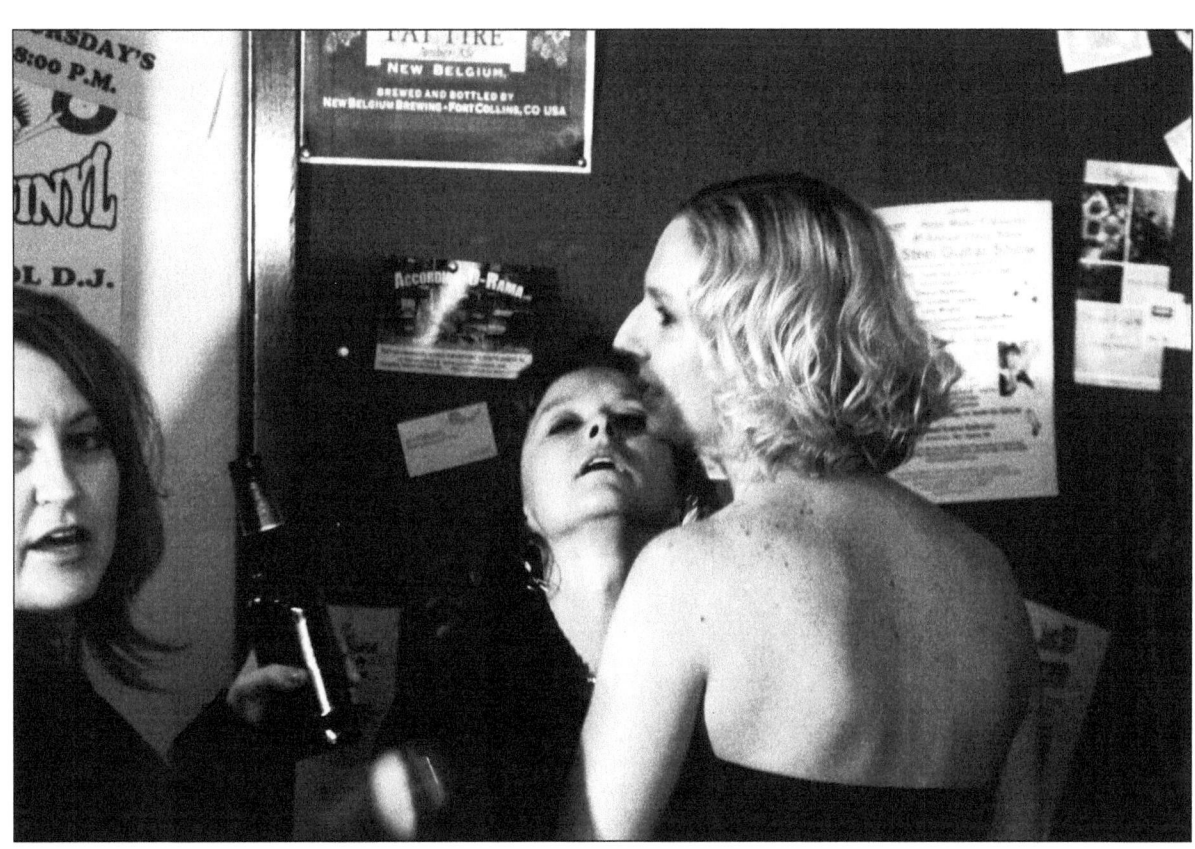

Country Music Guy With one of the Lost Boys

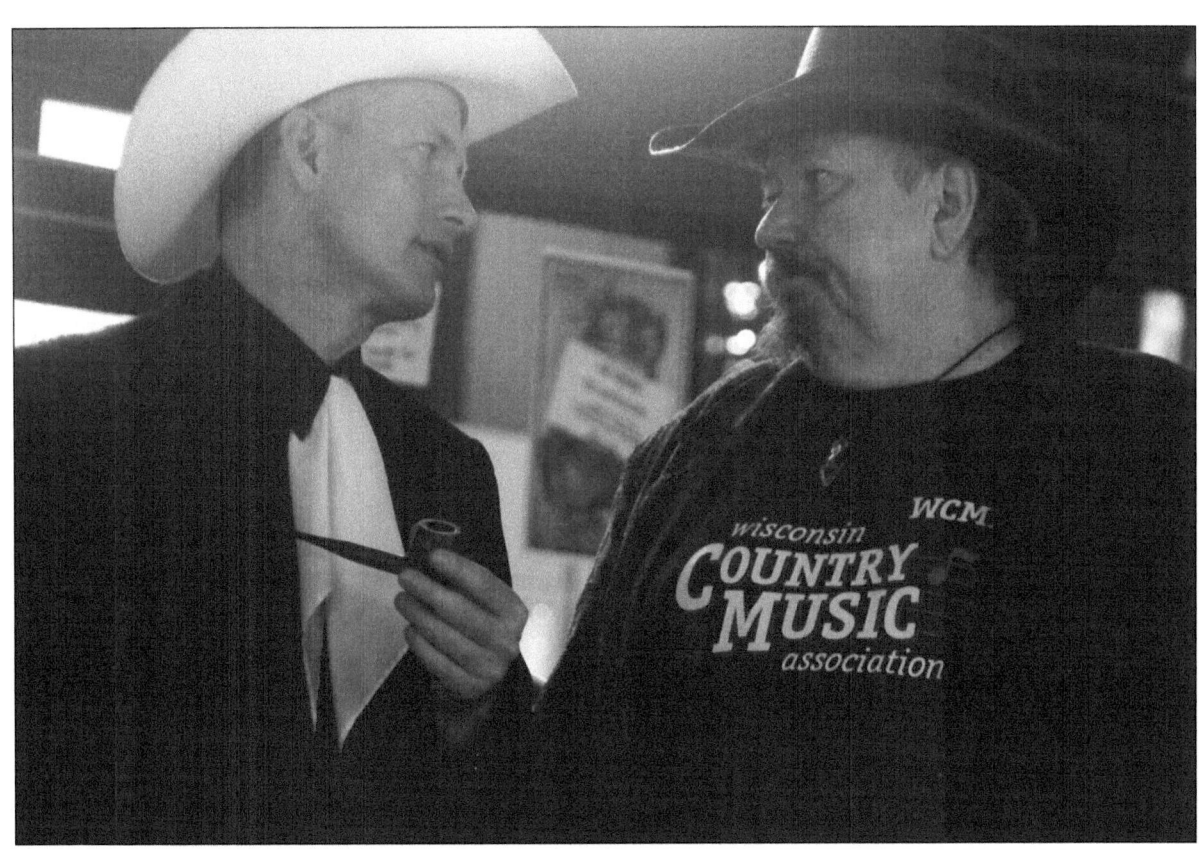

She Looks Kind of Sad

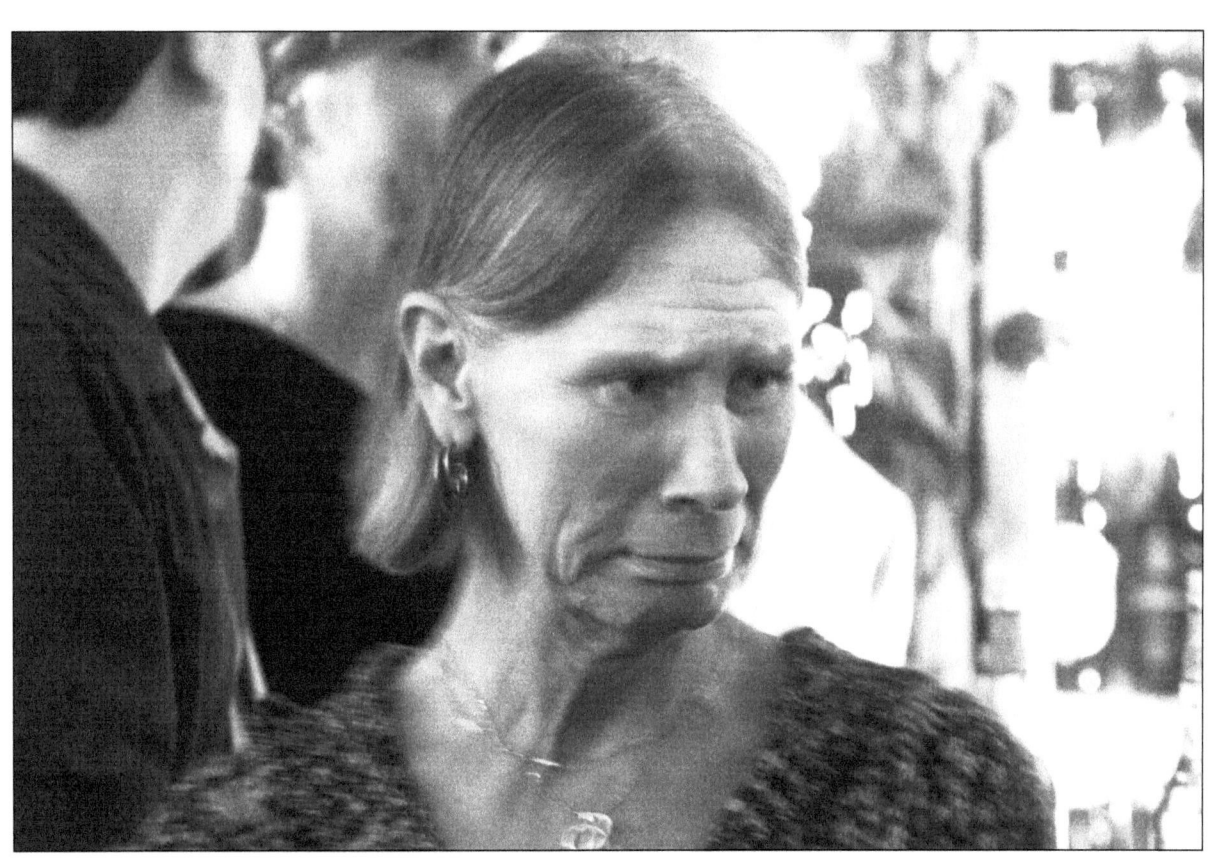

Blow!

"Big Al Groth" player from Reverend Raven
and the Chain Smokin' Alter Boys.

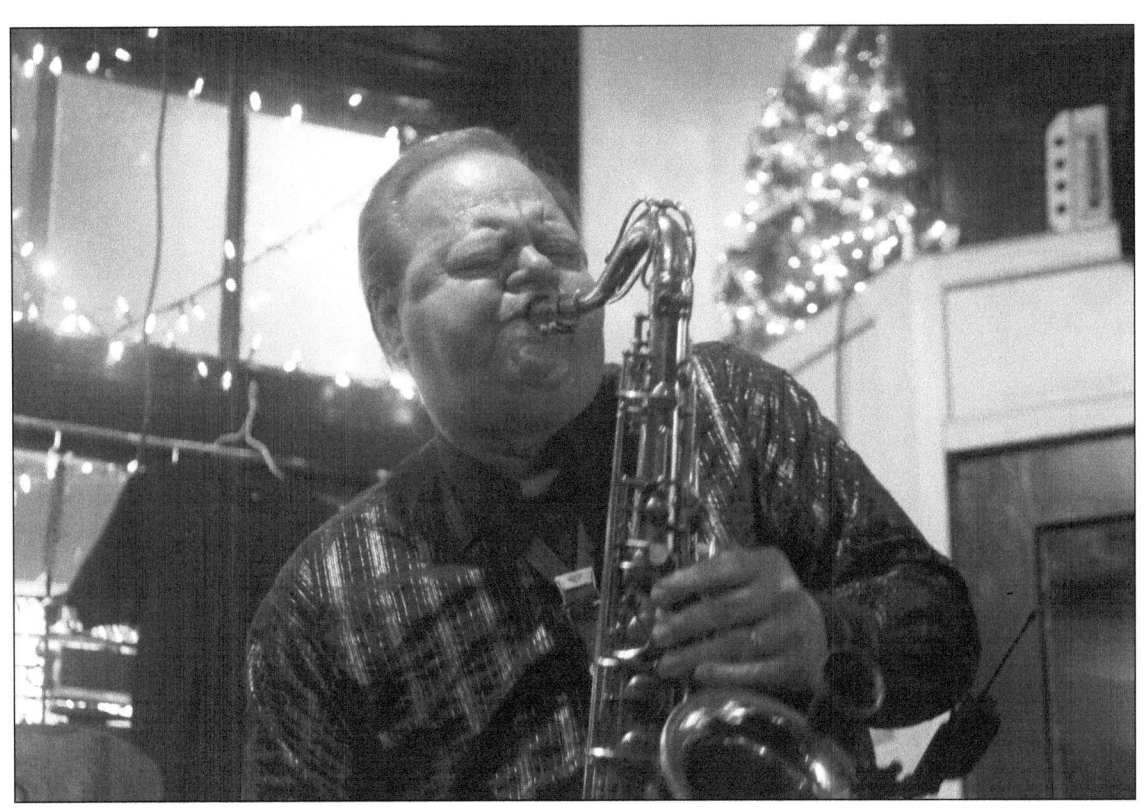

Andy Kochanski

Standing in front of his photo.

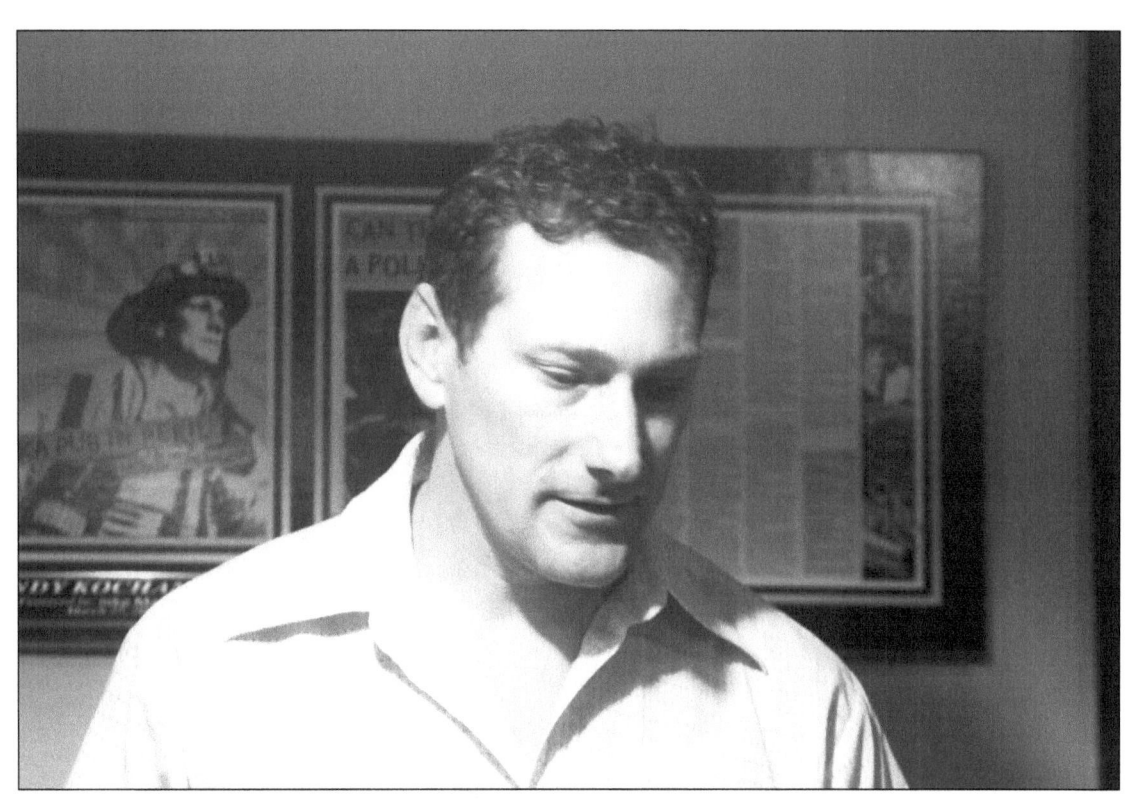

Closing Time

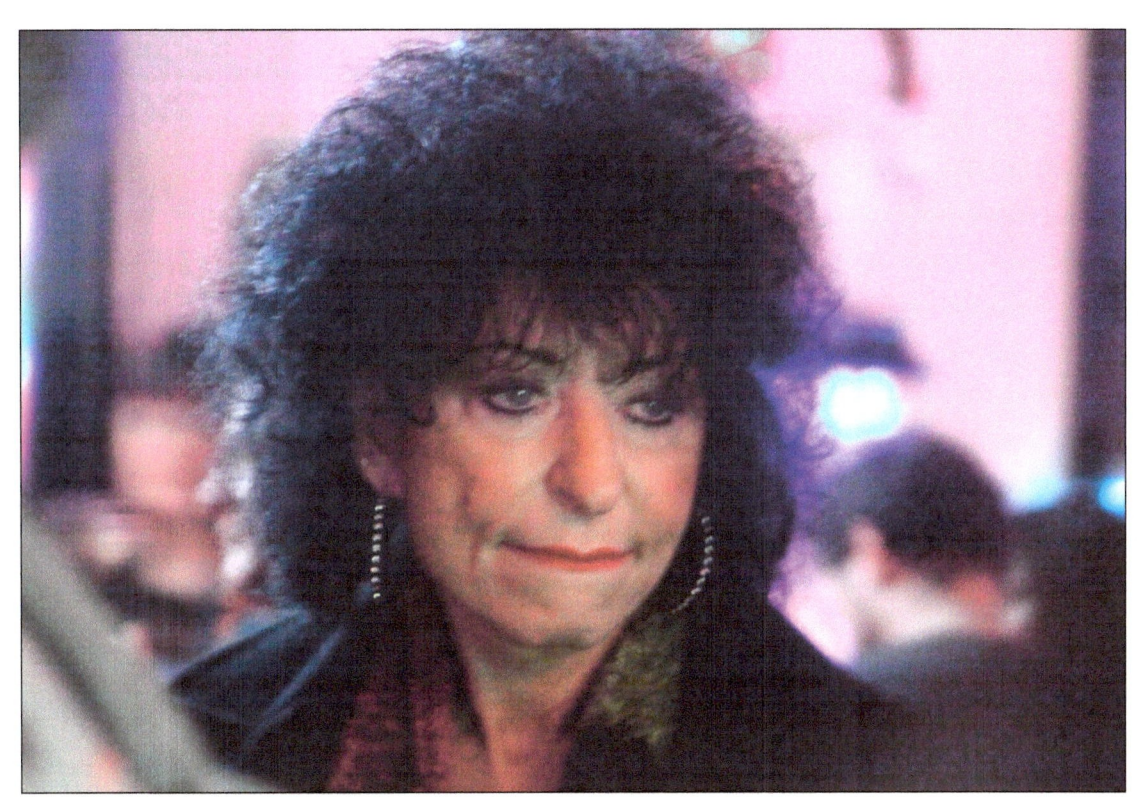

Photographer's Notes

These photos were taken over a four month period, during the winter of 2009–2010. The subject matter was a photographer's dream, the lighting was a photographers nightmare. The stage was illuminated by just a few dim, red light bulbs. Use of a flash was out of the question. It would have completely spoiled the atmosphere and have been entirely too disruptive. No film camera would have been sensitive enough to take a meaningful image in that almost cave-like setting, nor were any of my digital cameras sensitive enough for the assignment.

I sold my Canon Rebel to a friend and purchased a Canon 50D with an ISO capability of 32,000. (Ten-times more sensitive than a film camera or common digital cameras of that era.) For a few months at least I was "state of the art". By the time of this writing, that camera has become superannuated.

The first night in Kochanski's with the new camera I took well over 400 shots and came home quite excited. Once I viewed the images on my LCD screen I became horribly disappointed. Even with a sensitive camera, the images at first viewing appeared to be unusable. They were mostly red and washed out.

My initial disappointed turned to elation when I decided to do a minimal amount of photo-enhancement and simply convert the data to black & white, then increase the contrast as much as I deemed appropriate. The effect was exactly what I was looking for, the images have the appearance of sensitive but grainy 35mm film. Only a few of them had sufficient illumination for me to print in color. Since I started out over forty years ago with 35mm film and a dark room, my philosophy upon transition to digital has been to do not much more "processing" that what I could have done in a dark room.

www.ingramcontent.com/pod-product-compliance
Lightning Source LLC
Chambersburg PA
CBHW050744180526
45159CB00003B/1339